WORLD OF ANIMALS

SNAKES

BROWN BEAR BOOKS

BROWN BEAR BOOKS

Published by Brown Bear Books Limited

An imprint of
The Brown Reference Group plc
68 Topstone Road
Redding
Connecticut
06896
USA
www.brownreference.com

© 2008 The Brown Reference Group plc

This hardcover edition is distributed in the
United States by
Black Rabbit Books
P.O. Box 3263
Mankato, MN 56002

Library of Congress Cataloging-in-Publication Data
Somerville, Louisa.
 Snakes/ by Louisa Somerville.
    p. cm. -- (The world of animals)
 Includes index.
 Summary: "Describes the behavior, physical
    characteristics, and habitats of different
    species of snakes"--Provided by publisher.
 ISBN-13: 978-1-933834-32-0
1. Snakes--Juvenile literature. I. Title. II. Series.
QL666.O6S679 2009
597.96--dc22
                    2007049994

ISBN-13: 978-1-933834-32-0
ISBN-10: 1-933834-32-3

All rights reserved. This book is protected by copyright. No part of it may be reproduced, stored in a retrieval system, or transmitted in any form or by any means, without the prior permission in writing of the Publisher, nor be otherwise circulated in any form of binding or cover other than that in which it is published and without a similar condition including this condition being imposed on the subsequent publisher.

For the Brown Reference Group plc
Designer: Geoff Ward and Calcium
Editor: Louisa Somerville and Tim Harris
Creative Director: Jeni Child
Children's Publisher: Anne O'Daly
Editorial Director: Lindsey Lowe

Consultant

John P. Friel, Ph.D, Curator of Fishes, Amphibians
       & Reptiles, Cornell University Museum of
       Vertebrates, Ithaca, NY

Printed in the United States

Photographic credits:
Front Cover: NHPA: Stephen Dalton.
Ardea London Ltd: Jean-Paul Ferrero 27b, Geoff Trinder 9t; **Corbis:** Chris Mattison/Frank Lane Picture Library 9b, Joe McDonald 21; **NHPA:** Ken Griffiths 24, Daniel Heuclin 11b, Hellio Van Ingen 17t; **Nature Picture Library:** Peter Blackwell 29t, Georgette Douwma 15t, Mary McDonald 23t, Robert Valentic 3, 17b, 27t; **Oxford Scientific Films:** Tony Allen 23b, Mark Macewen 13t; **Shutterstock:** 5b, Brian J, Abela 11t, Ecoprint 4, Photobar 29b; **Still Pictures:** Kevin Aitken 14, James Geholdt 7t, Martin Harvey 5t, Andrew R. Odum 13b; **Superstock:** age fotostock 11c, 18,19t, David A. Northcott 6.

Contents

What Is a Snake? 4
Anaconda 6
Children's Python 8
Rainbow Boa 10
King Cobra 12
Sea Krait 14
Russell's Viper 16
Western Diamondback Rattlesnake 18
Sidewinder 20
Puff Adder 22
Taipan 24
Australian Tiger Snake 26
Mamba 28
Glossary 30
Further Resources 31
Index 32

Any words that appear in the text in bold, **like this**, are explained in the glossary.

What Is a Snake?

There are nearly 3,000 kinds of snakes, and they live on every continent except Antarctica. Nearly half of all **reptiles** are snakes! All snakes are meat eaters but not all produce **venom**.

The shape of a snake suits its lifestyle. For example, snakes that live in trees are usually long and thin to help them bridge the gap between branches. Burrowing snakes, on the other hand, often have a fat body and a short tail. Most snakes are dull in color, to blend in with surroundings such as dead leaves, sand, or mud. Snakes that live in trees may be green. Many kinds of snakes also have blotches, bands, or stripes that break up their outline and give them extra **camouflage**.

Although they do not have legs, snakes have no difficulty getting around. Most snakes move across the ground by wriggling their bodies from side to side in a series of S-shaped curves. Snakes use the same movement to swim. When a snake climbs up a rough tree trunk, it moves in another way. It first grips the tree with the front part of its body while the back half is pulled up. Next, it grips with the back half while the front half reaches forward.

Snakes have poor eyesight and hearing but an excellent sense of smell. They also use their tongues to pick up or "sense" chemicals in the air. The chemicals are passed to a special organ in the roof of their mouth. This happens when the snake draws its tongue back into the mouth.

Up Close

Some snakes have organs, called heat pits in their face. The pits pick up heat from **warm-blooded** animals, such as rats. The pits pinpoint the animal so that the snake can strike it, even in darkness.

Snakes' Scales

All snakes are covered in **scales**. The scales on a snake's back and sides are often smooth to help the snake slide over soil, sand, or water. When a snake sheds its "skin", it only removes the outer layer of the top part of its skin. The scales and their coloring remain on the snake.

This boa's scales have a dull pattern that helps keep the snake hidden from its enemies.

Anaconda

The green anaconda, found in South America, is the world's heaviest snake. It can kill a deer or a fully grown **caiman**. Only female anacondas reach truly enormous sizes.

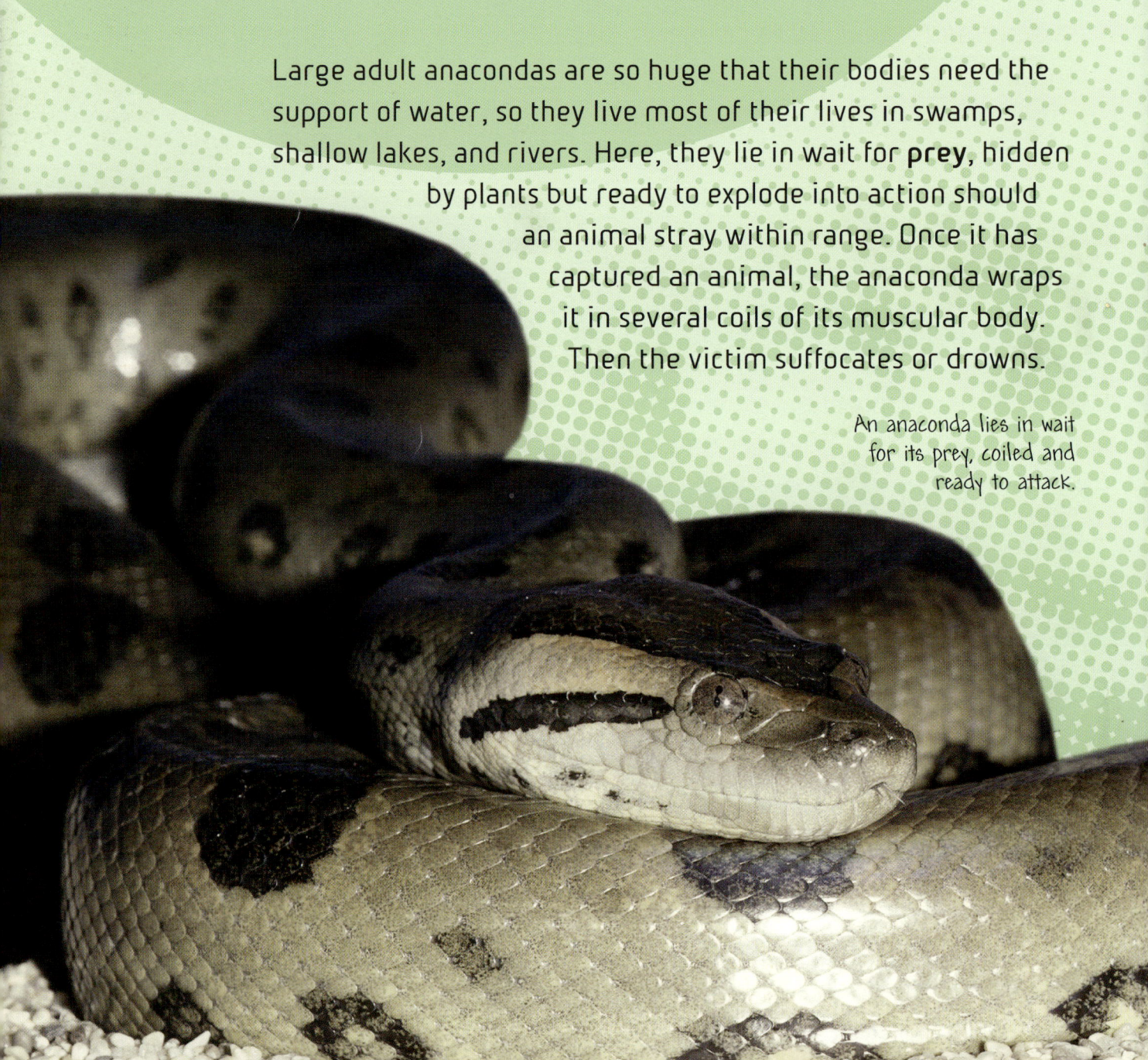

Large adult anacondas are so huge that their bodies need the support of water, so they live most of their lives in swamps, shallow lakes, and rivers. Here, they lie in wait for **prey**, hidden by plants but ready to explode into action should an animal stray within range. Once it has captured an animal, the anaconda wraps it in several coils of its muscular body. Then the victim suffocates or drowns.

An anaconda lies in wait for its prey, coiled and ready to attack.

UP CLOSE

An anaconda has a narrow head with both its eyes and its **nostrils** near the top. A bold black line runs diagonally backward from each of the anaconda's eyes to its jaw.

Mating Snakes

Anacondas usually mate in shallow water. A "ball" of up to 11 males crawl over one female, trying to mate with her. After mating, some female anacondas eat the males! But this is very rare.

Head

Tail

Scales

FACT FILE

Common name: anaconda

Scientific name: *Eunectes murinus*

Length: Up to 33 ft (10 m) or more

Key features: massive, greenish body with dark oval spots; thick neck; females more than twice as long as males

Diet: mammals (including deer, chickens, and dogs), birds, other reptiles; young anacondas eat fish and frogs as well

Children's Python

The Children's python of Australia is named not for its small size or because it would make a good pet! It is named for Dr. J. G. Children, a British zookeeper of the 1800s.

Children's pythons like to eat bats. They have a clever way to catch them in caves. First, the snake finds a place to hang from the roof of a cave. When the bats leave the cave in the evening, the snake lunges at them with its mouth open. As soon as it catches a bat, it coils around it, squeezes it tightly, and swallows it while still hanging from the roof!

FACT FILE

Common name: Children's python
Scientific name: Antaresia childreni
Length: can grow up to 3¼ ft (100 cm) long
Key features: small and slender with large yellow eyes; light brown body with lots of darker brown blotches on the back and sides
Diet: small mammals and birds; other reptiles

Tail
Eye
Scales

Up Close

A female Children's python lays a group, or clutch, of 6 to 12 eggs. She coils her body around the eggs and stays with them until they hatch.

Good Climbers

Children's pythons live in the far north of Australia. They live in many different places, including wet forests, open woodland, and deserts. They can even climb trees and rock faces.

As she keeps her eggs warm and safe, a female Children's python keeps a wary eye out for **predators**.

Rainbow Boa

The rainbow boa of Central and South America is a fairly slim but powerful snake with smooth, shiny **scales**. It is a secretive creature of the rain forest that hides by day and hunts at night.

The rainbow boa's head is narrow, and there are nearly always five dark lines running from the **snout** and down the head. The markings on the snake's back are black or dark brown oval rings. Sometimes the centers of the ovals are lighter in color, and some snakes have eyespots on their sides. The most colorful boas are the ones that live in the warm Amazon Basin.

Scales · Head · Snout · Tail

FACT FILE

Common name: rainbow boa
Scientific name: Epicrates cenchria
Length: from 5 ft (1.5 m) to 6½ ft (2 m)
Key features: powerful body with glossy scales
Diet: mostly **mammals**

Up Close

Some rainbow boas are covered in beautiful scales that shimmer with every color of the rainbow in sunlight. This is how the rainbow boa gets its name.

Rainbow boas can climb trees. This one is resting several feet off the ground.

Night Attack!

A rainbow boa hunts for food at night. On its snout are organs called heat pits. They pick up the heat given off by **warm-blooded** animals. This helps the snake find its **prey** in the dark.

Heat pit

A rainbow boa uses its heat pits to hunt down its dinner.

King Cobra

At twice the length of an average person, the king cobra is easily the longest poisonous snake in the world. Its closest rival in size is the black mamba.

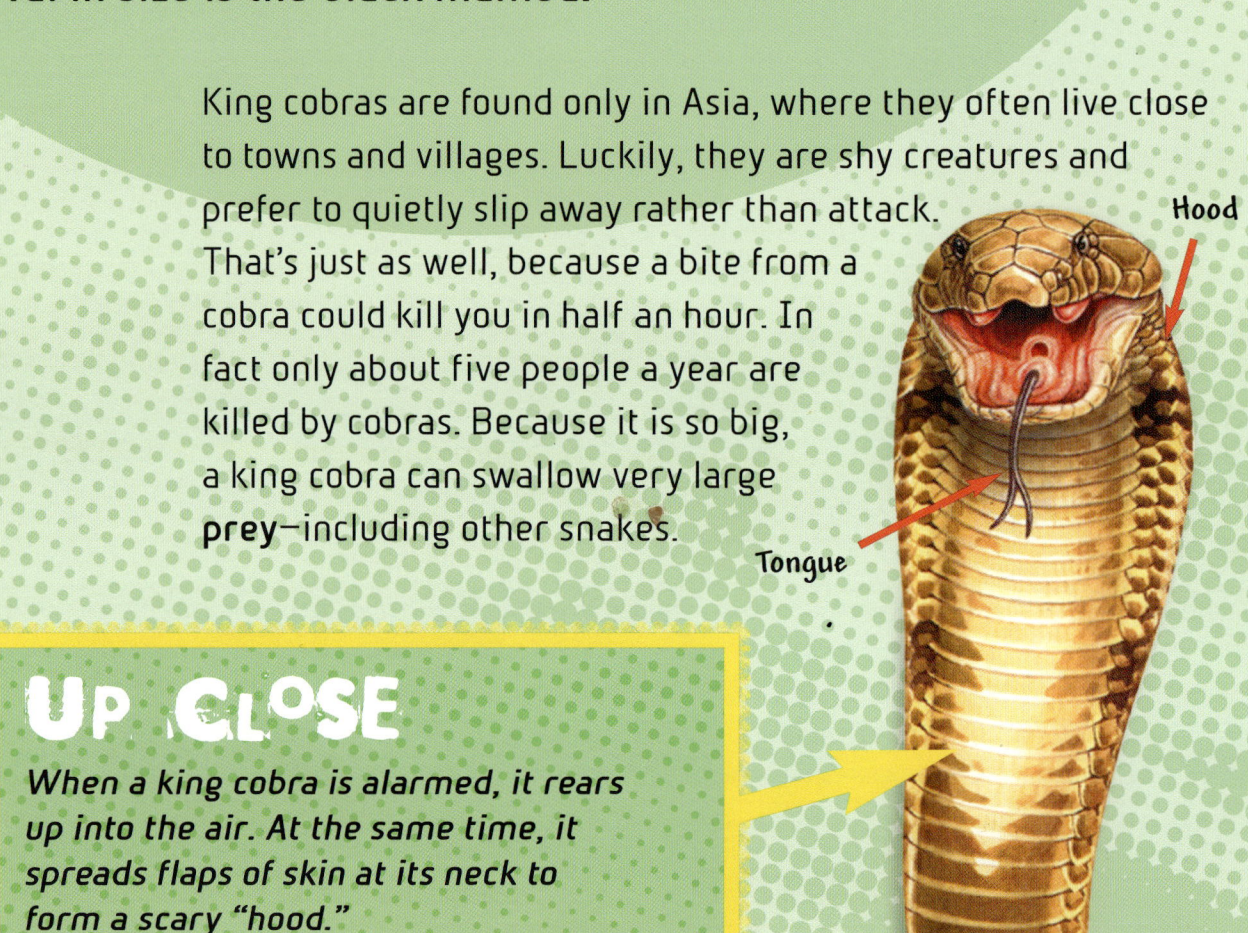

King cobras are found only in Asia, where they often live close to towns and villages. Luckily, they are shy creatures and prefer to quietly slip away rather than attack. That's just as well, because a bite from a cobra could kill you in half an hour. In fact only about five people a year are killed by cobras. Because it is so big, a king cobra can swallow very large **prey**—including other snakes.

Hood

Tongue

UP CLOSE

When a king cobra is alarmed, it rears up into the air. At the same time, it spreads flaps of skin at its neck to form a scary "hood."

Tail

Scales

As a king cobra raises its head to attack, it lets out a growling, low-pitched hiss.

FACT FILE

Common name: king cobra
Scientific name: Ophiophagus hannah
Length: usually grows from 10 ft (3 m) to 16½ ft (5m) but can reach 18 ft (5.5 m)
Key features: yellow or green body with smooth scales; spreads its long, narrow hood when it is threatened
Diet: other snakes, sometimes lizards

In The Nest

King cobras are the only snakes that build a nest. The female pulls together a pile of dead leaves with her coils. Then she lays 20 to 40 eggs. She guards the eggs from **predators**.

The eggs hatch after two months or so. The babies are already about 14 in (35 cm) long!

Sea Krait

The stripy sea krait lives in the **coral reefs** and coastal waters of Southeast Asia and Australia. It spends most of its time in the water, but it comes ashore to drink, mate, and lay its eggs.

Sea kraits eat mostly eels. The snakes hunt by cruising slowly over reefs, poking their head into holes. When a sea krait finds an eel, it pumps it with **venom**. Sometimes it bites the eel and then holds on until the poison takes effect. Other times it will let the eel go and track it down later, once the poison has worked. It may drag its **prey** onto land to eat it.

A sea krait glides over the coral reef in search of a tasty eel.

UP CLOSE

The bold black-and-white bands of color on a sea krait's body warn **predators** that the snake is poisonous and tastes nasty. Even a shark won't dare to attack a sea krait.

Safe In A Cave

A female sea krait lays six to 18 eggs at a time. She chooses a cave that is above the level of the sea so that the eggs don't get washed away. The young sea kraits hatch after about four or five months.

Head

Scales

Eel

Tail

FACT FILE

Common name:
sea krait

Scientific name:
Laticauda

Length: from 3 ft (91 cm) to 6½ ft (2 m)

Key features: cylinder-shaped body except for the tail, which is flattened; black and white in color, with rings around body and tail

Diet:
mostly eels

15

Russell's Viper

*Don't be fooled by the beautiful colors and patterns of the Russell's viper. More people are bitten by this **species** of snake than by either cobras or kraits.*

Russell's vipers live in South and Southeast Asia. They like to coil in the sun, well hidden among grasses and bushes. Their color and patterns provide good **camouflage**. From here they will **ambush** passing prey, but at night they set off to hunt. They go into villages and even into houses to look for rats to eat. If the snakes are threatened, they make a long, low hiss through their large **nostrils**.

Nostril   Head   Scales

Tail

FACT FILE

Common name: Russell's viper

Scientific name: *Daboia russelii*

Length: from 36 in (90 cm) to 5 ft (1.5 m) long

Key features: round, brown spots edged in black on body; dark stripe runs from eye to corner of jaw

Diet: mammals, such as rats, mice, and squirrels; birds, such as sparrows; lizards, and frogs

Strike Out!

Russell's vipers have heat-sensitive nerve endings in their faces. These can detect heat given off by **warm-blooded prey**, such as rats, mice, and birds. Once it has found its prey, the Russell's viper strikes with amazing speed. It launches an attack in the blink of an eye. It strikes so hard that it may even leave the ground as it hurls itself at the enemy!

Up Close

A viper's **fangs** can measure more than ½ inch (1.5 cm) long. The snake uses them to inject **venom** deep into a victim. It can pump enough poison in one bite to kill two people!

This Russell's viper may look as if it's resting—but it could attack at any second.

Western Diamondback Rattlesnake

The western diamond rattlesnake lives in the southwestern United States and Mexico. Its bite can cause serious injury, but it is easy to avoid if you listen out for its r-r-rattle!

Rattlesnakes don't use their rattles to confuse their **prey**, nor to attract other rattlesnakes! In fact, the rattle is like a bell that's rung to let other animals know the rattlesnake is close by. Huge herds of bison once roamed the plains of North America. Rattlesnakes shook their rattles to warn the bison they were there. The sound stopped the bison from trampling on them.

A western diamondback rattlesnake raises its rattle and shakes it from side to side.

Snake Snack!

The western diamondback rattlesnake lives in deserts, on rocky hillsides, and in other dry places—but only if there are enough small mammals to eat!

A rattlesnake's mouth opens incredibly wide as it strikes at a small **rodent**.

Up Close

A rattlesnake's rattle is made of keratin, a hard substance that also forms horn, nails, claws, and hair. The pieces of the rattle fit neatly one inside the other.

Rattle

Scales

Head

FACT FILE

Common name: western diamondback
Scientific name: Crotalus atrox
Length: From 2½ ft (76 cm) to 7 ft (2.1 m)
Key features: diamond-shaped markings along back of body; tail banded in black, ending in large segments (the rattle)
Diet: small mammals up to the size of young prairie dogs and rabbits

19

Sidewinder

The sidewinder is a kind of rattlesnake that is named for the way it moves. It slides sideways over loose desert sand. Only a small part of the snake's body touches the sand, so the animal can move more quickly.

Unlike most snakes, sidewinders don't have a home. They move across the desert each night, looking for lizards asleep in their burrows to eat. At daybreak, the snake shuffles down into the sand to escape the heat. It hides itself under a thin layer of sand so that it can surprise any **prey**, such as lizards or rats, that pass by.

Horn

UP CLOSE

The sidewinder has scales that bulge out above its eyes like a pair of horns. This is why some people call sidewinders "horned rattlesnakes."

Scales

Tail

Tricky Tails

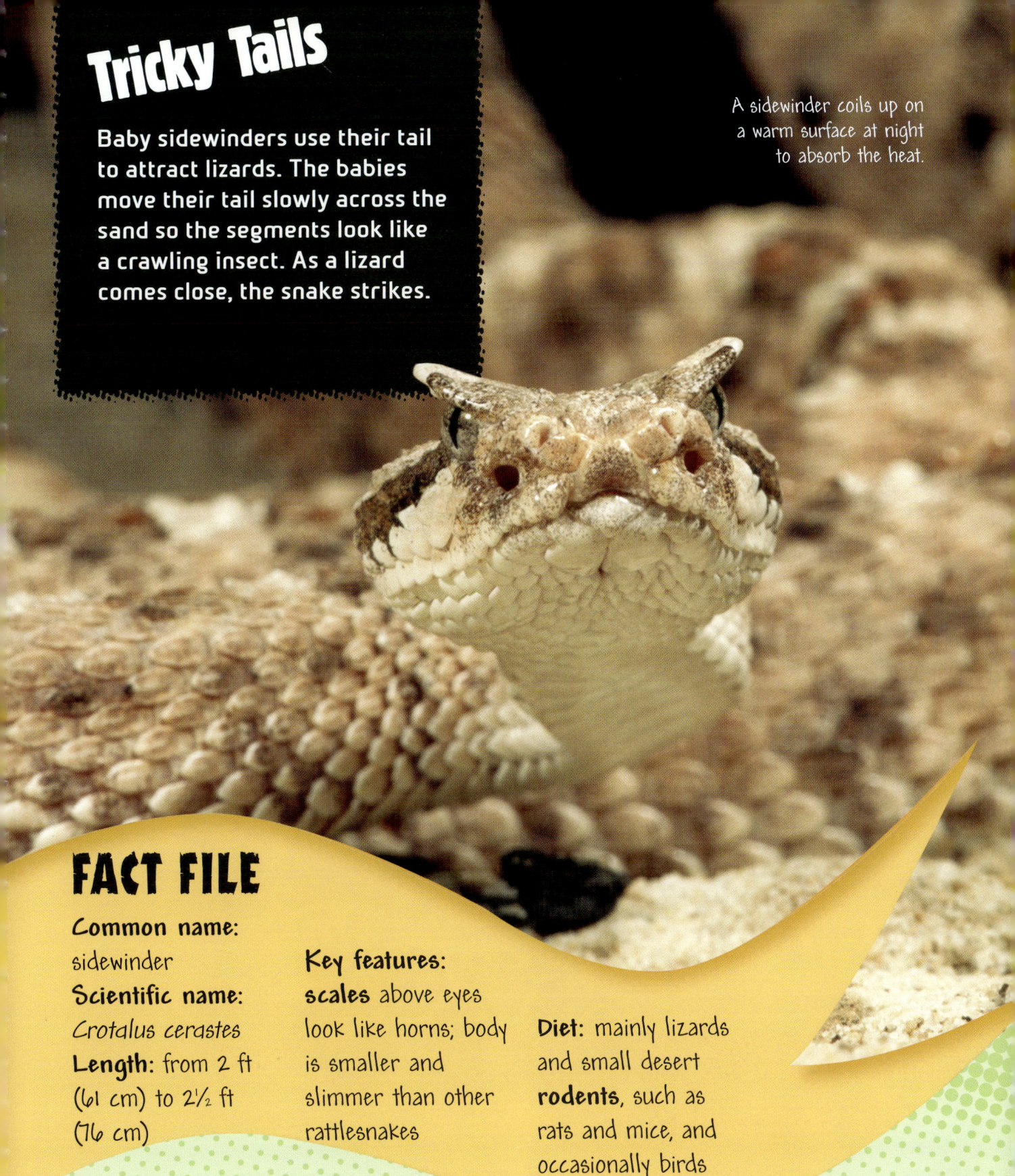

Baby sidewinders use their tail to attract lizards. The babies move their tail slowly across the sand so the segments look like a crawling insect. As a lizard comes close, the snake strikes.

A sidewinder coils up on a warm surface at night to absorb the heat.

FACT FILE

Common name: sidewinder

Scientific name: *Crotalus cerastes*

Length: from 2 ft (61 cm) to 2½ ft (76 cm)

Key features: **scales** above eyes look like horns; body is smaller and slimmer than other rattlesnakes

Diet: mainly lizards and small desert **rodents**, such as rats and mice, and occasionally birds

Puff Adder

The puff adder is a huge snake that lives in southern Africa. If it's scared, it puffs itself up by sucking air into its body. This makes it look bigger and more scary! The puff adder can also hiss very loudly to warn off an attacker.

An adult puff adder is so bulky that it cannot move from side to side like most snakes. Instead, it travels slowly in a straight line, like a caterpillar. The patterns on a puff adder's body help hide it from its **prey**. This snake hunts at dusk when it is harder for other animals to see it move. Puff adders often leap into the air as they strike a victim, and may even topple over backward.

Scales

Head

Mouth

FACT FILE

Common name: puff adder

Scientific name: Bitis arietans

Length: from 3 ft (90 cm) to 6 ft (1.8 m)

Key features: plump body; raised ridge on each scale; large, dark gray v-shaped marks along the back

Diet: birds, toads, lizards, and **mammals**, including small antelope and tortoises

Varied Diet

Puff adders eat rats, birds, toads, and other snakes. They will even eat African hedgehogs, and tortoises—which they swallow whole. The snake only injects **venom** into large prey.

UP CLOSE

A puff adder's **scales** are rough, with a raised ridge running along the middle. The ridges help the snake to grip surfaces and break up its outline. This makes it harder for prey to spot.

This puff adder's jaws are wide enough to tackle a large bird or even a hare.

Taipan

There are two kinds of taipans, and both are very poisonous. Some live around the coasts of Australia, and others live inland.

Taipans have very long **fangs**. They use them to bite their **prey**. Poisonous **venom** is squirted through the fangs and into their victim. A bite from a taipan contains more than enough venom to kill several humans or many smaller animals! Despite this, taipans are shy and rarely bite people. They hunt mostly in the morning. Then, they seek out prey in holes, burrows, and deep cracks in dried mud.

After the wet season, an inland taipan looks for prey in cracks in the dried-up mud.

UP CLOSE

Both kinds of taipans have a very fast and accurate bite. This means that a taipan can quickly inject its deadly venom into its victim and kill it.

Poison Power

Inland taipans are the most **venomous** land snakes of all. A single bite can inject enough poison to kill 200,000 mice. That's 50 times more mice than could be killed by an Indian cobra!

Head

Tail

Scales

FACT FILE

Common name: taipan

Scientific name: Oxyuranus

Length: 6½ ft (2 m) to 12 ft (3.6 m)

Key features: large tube-shaped body; narrow head; usually some shade of brown in color

Diet: mammals, mostly the plague rat, one of the few **rodents** in the dry Australian desert

25

Australian Tiger Snake

The Australian mainland tiger snake is one of the most **venomous** snakes in the world. But although some people are bitten by tiger snakes each year, very few people actually die.

When a tiger snake is annoyed, it flattens its neck and raises its head off the ground like a cobra does. And it will bite if it gets the chance. However, a tiger snake's bite is unlikely to kill you. Its poison can be treated with **antivenin**. Most people don't take any chances, though: they wear clothes that cover their legs.

Tail

Head

UP CLOSE

Tiger snakes swallow frogs whole, without waiting for their **venom** to work. However, a tiger snake will release larger **prey** (such as a rat) after biting it. The snake will then follow the dying animal and eat it later.

Scales

26

FACT FILE

Common name: Australian tiger snake

Scientific name: *Notechis scutatus*

Length: from 4 ft (1.2 m) to 7 ft (2.1 m)

Key features: plump body with large **scales**; large head with a blunt nose and small eyes

Diet: mostly frogs; also lizards, birds, and small **mammals**, such as rats

Snake Sizes

A tiger snake's size depends on the size of its diet! Large ones eat big seabirds and rats. Medium-sized snakes eat smaller seabirds and mice. And the smallest tiger snakes eat small lizards.

A hungry tiger snake waits for a lizard to move a little closer.

Mamba

Mambas are aggressive snakes that attack at lightning speed. One kind of mamba, the black mamba, is the fastest snake there is. And mambas are also very **venomous**.

Several kinds of mambas live in Africa. Some live high in trees and are rarely seen. The black mamba lives in piles of rocks, hollow tree trunks, or termite mounds on the plains. Luckily, mambas are secretive snakes and prefer to hide rather than attack people.

Head

Tree

Tail

FACT FILE

Common name: mamba
Scientific name: Dendroaspis
Length: from 5 ft (1.5 m) to 14 ft (4.3 m)

Key features: long, slim body with smooth **scales**; can be green, gray, or brown; never black except inside mouth

Diet: rodents, bats, birds, especially baby birds

Open Wide!

A mamba often moves with its head and neck held high. If threatened, it can lift half its body off the ground and spread a narrow "hood" around its neck. Then it opens its mouth wide and hisses.

This green mamba moves at great speed through the trees. The ground-dwelling black mamba can move even faster, though.

Up Close

A black mamba has a long head with straight sides. Its head and body are covered in smooth scales. The black mamba's dark coloring helps it to stay hidden in rocks and hollow tree trunks.

Glossary

ambush To attack suddenly from a hidden place.

antivenin A substance made from snake venom that is used to treat snake bites.

caiman A kind of crocodile that lives in the tropical parts of the Americas. Caimans are closely related to alligators.

camouflage A coloring or body shape that helps an animal to blend with—and hide in—its surroundings.

coral reef A line of coral that lies below the water in warm, shallow seas. Coral is made up of tiny animals.

fang A long, pointed tooth. Some snakes use their fangs to inject venom.

mammal An animal that is warm-blooded and feeds its young on its own milk. Most mammals also have hair or fur.

nostril An opening in the nose through which an animal or person breathes.

predator An animal that hunts other animals for food.

prey An animal that is hunted by another animal.

reptile An animal with a scaly skin. A reptile is cold blooded, which means that its temperature varies with its surroundings.

rodent A small mammal, such as a rat or mouse, with large teeth.

scales Tough, waterproof coverings that grow out of a snake's skin. The scales protect the snake's body while letting it stretch and bend.

snout An animal's nose and jaws.

species A group of animals that share features, and can mate and produce young together.

venom A poisonous liquid that some snakes produce. They inject the poison into their victims by biting with their fangs.

venomous An animal that produces venom.

warm-blooded An animal that can keep its body at about the same temperature all the time. People, rats, and birds are all warm blooded.

Further Resources

Books about snakes

Under My Feet: Snakes by Patricia Whitehouse, Raintree Publishers, 2004
In the Wild: Snakes by Claire Robinson, Heinemann Library, 2001
Snakes by Sally Morgan, QED Publishing, 2005
Snakes by Claire Llewellyn, OUP, 2000
Scary Creatures: Snakes by Penny Clarke, Book House, 2002

Useful websites

www.kidsplanet.org/factsheets/snakes.htm
www.worldalmanacforkids.com
cybersleuth-kids.com/sleuth/Science/Animals/Reptiles/Snakes
www.enchantedlearning.com
www.wc4.org/reptiles_snakes.htm

Index

ambush 16, 30
anaconda 6–7
antivenin 26, 30
Australian tiger snake 26–27

baby snakes 7, 13, 15, 21, 25, 28
bats 8
birds 8, 16, 17, 21, 22, 23, 27, 28
bison 18

caiman 6, 30
camouflage 5, 16, 30
Children's python 8–9
cobra 16, 25, 26
colors 5, 16
coral reef 14, 30

desert 9, 20

eels 14
eggs 9, 13, 14, 15, 25
eyes 7, 8, 10, 14, 21, 27

fangs, 17, 24, 30

head 7, 10, 13, 14, 25, 26, 27
heat pits 5, 11
hiss 13, 16, 22, 29
hood 12, 13, 29

jaw 7, 16, 23

keratin 19
king cobra 12–13

mamba 12, 28–29
mammal 7, 8, 10, 16, 19, 22, 25, 27, 30
mate 7, 14

nest 13
nostrils 7, 16, 30

patterns 16, 22
poison 4, 12, 14, 15, 17, 24, 25, 26, 28
predator 5, 9, 13, 15, 30
prey 6, 11, 12, 14, 16, 17, 18, 20, 22, 23, 24, 26, 30
puff adder 22–23

rainbow boa 10–11
rats 5, 16, 17, 20, 21, 23, 25, 26, 27
reptile 4, 7, 8, 30
rodent 19, 21, 25, 29, 31
Russell's viper 16–17

scales 5, 10, 11, 13, 21, 23, 27, 31
sea krait 14–15
sidewinder 20–21
snout 10, 11, 31
species 4, 16, 31

tail 5, 11, 19, 21
taipan 24–25
tongue 5
trees 4, 9, 11, 28, 29

venom 14, 17, 23, 24, 25, 26, 31

warm-blooded animals 5, 11, 17, 31
western diamondback rattlesnake 18–19